Sri Aurobindo's Vedanta: The Rhythm of Ananda

Sushrut Badhe

Published by Midam Charitable Trust

आनन्दमयं जगदिदं सर्वमं परब्रम्हणामवर्तितम् ।
मायाऽपि परवब्रम्हः प्रसान्तस्य सान्त रूपिणम्॥

This world is replete with consciousness of bliss,
From the Brahman supreme, it has descended
Maya too is (part of) the Brahman supreme,
A finite form of the infinite.

CONTENTS

ACKNOWLEDGMENT

To Sri Madhusudan Damle ji, for accepting a complete fool as his *shishya.* 12 years have passed like 12 seconds under your watchful care, Sir.

To the heroes who will be the harbingers of the 'Consciousness revolution'. I will consider myself blessed if I get to see you in my life time. Even if I don't, I sincerely pray – "*Come soon, dear ones. The world is crying out for divine love.*"

FOREWORD

Why must one read a book like this? My answer is, out of the dire need to save oneself. The underlying reason behind the increasing number of people getting angry, cynical, and restless is their disconnect with their cultural inheritance – something they can't even acknowledge. Humanity evolved itself very rapidly and extensively by understanding the vastness of the universe and the laws by which it is governed. I consider Sri Aurobindo, a brilliant student, administrator, philosopher, and a yogi, the last of the rishis delivering the divine intelligence bestowed upon humanity by the Supreme Creator. When the author, a young man in his early thirties and a mechanical engineer by education, whose parents were doctors, approached me with this work, I was taken aback by the strange way certain things happen in this world. We have been connected through Dr. APJ Abdul Kalam, with whom I spent 33 years of my working life, and whom he idolized, but I am yet to meet him in person.

I too am a mechanical engineer and my philosophical leanings have come through Dr. Kalam. He was a devout Muslim, educated in Christian missionary schools, and published a book on his spiritual experiences with Pramukh Swamiji, the spiritual head of BAPS, Bochasanwasi Akshar Purushottam Swaminarayan Sanstha, a Hindu denomination within the Swaminarayan Sampradaya. There is no doubt whatsoever in my mind that all religions served well in giving humanity a structured way to live and flourish. I do not see any contradiction between religion and science. What the ancient people imagined as gods and daemons were later defined by science as natural and psychological forces. But as science kept discovering many of these forces, each discovery led to newer unknowns.

As religion has gone out of fashion, especially among the urbane and the savvy, people by and large have lost touch with their bearings. Even outwardly religious people are mostly practising dogmas devoid of genuine faith. This disconnect is not without consequences. There is a pandemic of lifestyle diseases among the young. Even grown-ups appear confused and sit in front of TVs with numb minds and wither away their cognitive energy in the ever-open vanity fair of this world. This book from an engineer, from a Puducherry elite, comes as a fresh breeze. I consider writing this Foreword as my share of the good fortune and bliss of being part of a divine task.

Sri Aurobindo has written about all the major *Upanishads* and his translations are available on the Internet as the most authentic version for people not knowing Sanskrit, the language in which these were originally written. The *Sri Aurobindo Upanishad*, considered a personal message of Sri Aurobindo, is pivoted around the idea of s*at-chit-ananda*, which is indeed a universal idea. This is similar to the description of God as Ibn 'Arabi's *wahdat al-wujûd* and St. Augustine's *summo meo* (beyond my utmost heights), but also interior (*intimo meo)* —more inward to me than my innermost depths.

Reading the poetic rendering of the *Sri Aurobindo Upanishad* in English resonates with *Centuries of Meditations*, written by Thomas Traherne (1636-1674). He graduated from Oxford before becoming a priest in the Church of England, or the Anglican Church. He died at a young age of 37, after writing some 510 paragraphs, calling each 100 paragraphs a "century." For over 200 years, this manuscript survived in neglect as a bundle of scribbled papers.

As goes the legend, a connoisseur found them in a street book stall for sale as trash and the book was published in 1908. Later, the celebrated English writer, C. S. Lewis (1898–1963), called *Centuries of Meditations* "almost the most beautiful book in English." Like the *Sri Aurobindo Upanishad*, *Centuries of Meditations* revolves around the concept of "felicity," the state of bliss, as its thematic axis. Thomas Traherne writes:

That all the World is yours, your very senses and the inclinations of your mind declare. The Works of God manifest, His laws testify, and His word Both prove it. His attributes most sweetly make it evident. The powers of your soul confirm it. So that in the midst of such rich demonstrations, you may infinitely delight in God as your Father, Friend and Benefactor, in yourself as His Heir, Child and Bride, in the whole World, as the Gift and Token of His love; neither can anything, but Ignorance destroy your joys.[1]

So, it is ignorance – in our separateness, or isolation, anger and fear – that insulate us from the natural and innate feeling of the joy of living, called *joie de vivre* by the French people, for a cheerful enjoyment of life, an exultation of spirit – be it the joy of conversation, the joy of eating, the joy of anything one might do. Am I not happy writing this note, or are you not happy reading it? Whatever is done with joy as a base is good, promotes goodness, and multiplies joy in the process.

The *Taittiriya Upanishad* (III.6.1) declares:

आनन्दो ब्रह्मेति व्यजानात्

Know that bliss is eternal (Brahman)
आनन्दाध्येव खल्विमानि भूतानि जायन्ते

All beings are born of bliss
आनन्दं प्रयन्त्यभि संविशन्तीति

Enjoy themselves in bliss and dissolve (in bliss).

The concept of *ananda* is also central to the Hindu religion. In the Sri Ramakrishna Mission Order, it is very common for saints to have *ananda* as their part of their ordained name as monks, the most celebrated monk being Swami Vivekananda (1863-1902).

Sri Aurobindo declares *ananda* as the default state of creation. Bliss is better understood as a state of tranquillity; an equilibrium, a poise, a silence between two musical notes, those brief moments when your breath becomes air coming in and going out without you being aware of inhaling and exhaling it, a great harmony between all that exists.

[1] https://www.ccel.org/ccel/traherne/centuries.html. Last accessed on November 19, 2022. (I. 16)

There are 19 aphorisms in the *Sri Aurobindo Upanishad*. The author thoughtfully divided it into four movements. The first six aphorisms, devoted to the principles of Cosmic (*Brahmic*) Consciousness, are called the first movement. Sri Aurobindo takes a stance diametrically opposite to ब्रह्म सत्यं जगन्मिथ्या जीवो ब्रह्मैव नापरः, Brahman is truth, the universe is false, the living entity is Brahman alone, and there is no other of Adi Shankaracharya. He declares जगत् अपि ब्रह्म तत्सत्यं न मिथ्या, the universe is also Brahman, that is true and not false.

There is One Reality, complete, as narrated in this famous shloka mentioned in multiple Upanishads.

ॐ पूर्णमदः पूर्णमिदं पूर्णात्पूर्णमुदच्यते ।
पूर्णस्य पूर्णमादाय पूर्णमेवावशिष्यते ॥[2]
That (seen and unseen outer world) is full, this (unseen inner world) is full, from one fullness everything emerges
The full takes from the full and the full remains.

The next four aphorisms are called the second movement, describing the apparent God present everywhere in the Creation. This movement uses the logic of the sun to prove the first movement and nudges us to feel the presence of sun up in the sky in the warmth and light falling upon the earth.

सः तु सतः सत्यप्रकाशः तथा इह जगद्ब्रह्म भगवतः ...[3]
As the light is the Sun, similarly, this world is the Divine.

Aphorisms 11 to 16 are called the third movement, the dual world is presented as two aspects of one. Darkness has no separate existence except absence of light. All duality is two ends of one coin.

अज्ञानं ज्ञानस्य क्रीडा स्वस्मिन् आत्मगोपनं दौर्वल्यां शक्तेः क्रीदा निरानन्दम् आनन्दस्य क्रीडा स्वात्मनि आत्मगोपनम् ॥[4]
Like ignorance is the play of knowledge, what is shown is merely an aspect of what remains concealed. Like weakness is the realization of

---

[2] https://greenmesg.org/stotras/vedas/om_purnamadah_purnamidam.php
[3] https://upanishads.org.in/upanishads/10/8
[4] https://upanishads.org.in/upanishads/10/13

the absence of power. Thus absence of bliss a cue to feel bliss as the concealment of itself in itself.

Isha Upanishad (verse 9) cautions about the ignorance of this one reality and trying to know this world as something other than the Divine. This life is to feel and not to think about.

अन्धन्तमः प्रविशन्ति येऽविद्यामुपासते ।
ततो भूय इव ते तमोय उ विद्यायां रताः॥[5]
Those who are ignorant enter the darkness.
In deeper darkness go those who are engaged in learning.

The final three aphorisms are called the fourth movement, the destiny of creation – experiencing bliss.

भगवता आदिष्टः हि आनन्दं प्रवक्षामि।
As commanded by the Divine, I shall indeed expound the Bliss.[6]

Divinity is present right here in this world. Emphasizing the sanctity of that exists, Sri Aurobindo Upanishad calls for feeling the *ananda* which is the essence of the Creation.

My heartfelt gratitude to the author for writing this book and respectful thanks to Shri Madhusudan Damleji for grooming the author for undertaking this quality and value of task.

I offer this book to the readers with a prayer from आनन्दलहरी composed by Shri Adi Shankaracharya (Verse 12):

अयः स्पर्शे लग्नं सपदि लभते हेमपदवीं
यथा रथ्यापाथः शुचि भवति गंगौघमिलितम्।
तथा तत्तत्पापैरतिमलिनमन्तर्मम यदि
त्वयि प्रेम्णा सक्तं कथमिव न जायेत विमलम्॥[7]

---

[5] https://shlokam.org/texts/ishavasya-9/
[6] https://upanishads.org.in/upanishads/10/19
[7] https://hi.wikipedia.org/wiki/आनन्दलहरी (Verse 12)

Like the philosopher's stone turns metal into gold, water in the gutters turn good upon joining the river Ganga, so also, a mind devoted to God receives bliss. Bliss is thus contagious.
Mind your breath, listen to your heartbeat, feel your thoughts appearing and disappearing as clouds in the sky, and you can taste the bliss already within you.

Arun Tiwari
www.aruntiwari.com

Hyderabad
November 2022

Author's note

Seven years ago, I was a fool and so I rendered the Upanishad of Sri Aurobindo into a poem. Today, I am a bigger fool and so am daring to re-publish the same with a commentary.

In Sanskrit, a literary work that is a combination of prose and poetry is called a *Champu kavya* and I am attempting a brief *Champu kavya* in English on this Sanskrit text written by Sri Aurobindo during his initial years of stay in Pondicherry between 1910-1914. Sri Aurobindo himself did not translate his Sanskrit work nor did he give it a title. It was in 1978 that Pt. Jagannath Vedalankar, a renowned Sanskrit scholar at the Sri Aurobindo Ashram, translated the text into English and the same was published in the journal- *Sri Aurobindo: Archives and Research.*

The title "Sri Aurobindopanishad" along with the prose order and meaning was published in 1987 by the Sanskrit Karyalaya of the Sri Aurobindo Ashram Publication Department.

I, with whatever little lived experience I have accumulated in this birth, have come to understand that even foolish occurrences sometimes have a divine orderliness which is at play behind the scheme of things. And as I was completing this book, I came across some very interesting incidents that can be best described with only one word- serendipity.

Sometime in between 1988-1989, even before I was born, one fine morning, an elderly man wearing a shirt and dhoti entered 'Zamindar garden', which was then the home of my Guru, Sri Madhusudan Damle. His door was always open for all but as the unexpected guest entered the home, Damleji was surprised to see him. He looked at the gentlemen and asked him-
"Who do you wish to meet. What work do you have?"

The elderly man simply replied – "I don't know why I came here. I was searching for something. But after coming here, I saw the picture of Mother and Sri Aurobindo and so I just came. Can I have a glass of water?"
Damleji then gladly offered his guest water and asked him what his name was to which he replied – "I am Jagannath Vedalankar. I work for the Sanksrit department" and then he simply walked away. When Damleji enquired with a student from the ashram who had just joined him, he came to know that his guest was a good *sadhak* and scholar who worked at the ashram's Sanskrit department. The two never met each other again.

Twenty six years later, in 2015, for the first *Yog Diwas*- International Yoga Day, Damleji's students from Maharashtra were going to visit him with their children who were incidentally, also his students. For their benefit, Damleji felt Sri Aurobindopanishad would be ideal for their reading session and as his students were more comfortable in their mother tongue, Damleji translated the book into Marathi for all of them and this inspired me to immediately attempt the poetic rendition of the same.

Now in 2022, as I was approached by Gayatri Majumdar, the director of the Pondicherry/ Auroville Poetry festival and presented with an opportunity to officially release the book, I felt inspired to re-furbish my previously written poem and publish the same by dressing it with a brief prosaic commentary and some other relevant poems that I believe will enrich the reading experience.

And with this little story, I have successfully tried to present to you a fool's rationale on why I have written this book. I am completely in awe of Sri Aurobindo's Upanishad as in a nutshell, the great master has presented to us His Vedanta. I hope you find it worth your precious time.

- **Sushrut Badhe,**
14 November 2022

Understanding Sri Aurobindo

The layman considers matter and spirit to be antipodes and mutually exclusive. But are the two really so different? This question arises in almost every mind which has an inkling to understand the philosophy of life, nature and existence. Aldous Huxley's *"The Perennial Philosophy"* is a must read prescription offered by teachers, both in the east and west, for every student of philosophy. But as one sifts through the pages of the book, in the chapter which prods the reader to recognize the god in the world, we see a quote of Sri Aurobindo from his seminal work –Life divine, which is also prominently featured in his book recommendations

"The touch of Earth is always reinvigorating to the son of Earth, even when he seeks a supraphysical Knowledge. It may even be said that the supraphysical can only be really mastered in its fullness — to its heights we can always reach — when we keep our feet firmly on the physical. 'Earth is His footing,' says the Upanishad whenever it images the Self that manifests in the universe."

- *Sri Aurobindo*

These words echo a sentiment that beats in every sensitive heart that does not feel the entire world to be a complete illusion, as proposed by various religious schools that claim that the truth of the creator doesn't exist in the creation. But it won't be wrong to question either as to how one could actually materialize such a truth which is perfect in a world of imperfection and lies.

The Upanishad, mentioned in the quote refers to a body of ancient Indian scriptures, that is the foundation of the great philosophy of *Vedanta* that predates all the religions of the world.

The Vedantic schools of philosophy that spawned from the inspirations drawn from various Upanishadic texts, all sought to identify the way to realizing the highest cognizable truth which they called the *Brahman* – the Self. Owing to the metaphysical nature of the mystic texts, interpretations of the Brahman varied from school to school prominently categorized into the schools of *Dvaita, Advaita* and *Vishistadwaita* based upon their perception of *Brahman* as Dual, non-Dual and Qualified non-dualism. While disciples of the various schools often opposed each other's interpretations in approaching the Brahman, at times engaging in vociferous debates, all were of the common agreement that this great truth is hidden behind, what we may call a matrix of illusion, which they termed as Maya. Only those who were consciously awake and vigilant could free themselves from the trap of Maya and understand the great supraphysical truth- Brahman. The Isha Upanishad declared this truth to be beyond the dualities, beyond knowledge and ignorance, vidya and avidya, while the Manudkya postulated that this truth needs to be experienced in the fourth dimension that it considered to be the realm of the Atman-the spirit within, and that it was in a silent oneness that this Brahman could be realized – shantam shivam advaitam, chaturtham manyante, sa atma sa vignyeyaha.

While the paths and approaches of the Upanishads were different, the objective was one- to attain the Bramhaviyda or gnosis of the *Brahman*. The Upanishads adopted different styles to capture the elusive and all pervading Brahman, either as a story- *Kathopanishad*, questions- *Prashnopanishad*, riddles- *Kenopanishad*, exhaustive analysis of a hypothesis on the *Brahman- Brihadarnyaka* Upanishad etc. The Upanishads are themselves quite explicitly clear about their truths, but the interpretations often leave behind plenty of grey areas. One set of interpretations took prominence and overtook all others, and this led to the drawing of a thick line between matter and spirit. It was a general understanding, which many do have even today, that what was material couldn't be spiritual and vice versa. This is where we turn to Sri Aurobindo.

Enter Sri Aurobindo and all the grey areas disappear. In his light, the line that demarcates matter from spirit simply vanishes.

The Spirit shall look out through Matter's gaze
And Matter shall reveal the Spirit's face.
Then man and superman shall be at one
And all the earth become a single life.
Sri Aurobindo – Savitri: CWSA, Vol. 34, Book Eleven, p. 709

Only a rigid subscription to the rejectionist approach to the world, would make one fall into a misconception that Sri Aurobindo's approach and perspective is different from the Shastras. Sri Aurobindo did not digress from what the Vedic Rishis postulated, he took their works of the Vedanta & Veda further ahead, unlocking the secrets of the Veda establishing the pshychological functioning of the various Vedic Gods in the world. His emphasis on a terrestrial realization of the supraphysical truth, is in perfect accordance with the Upanishadic texts, the Veda and also in resonance with Sri Krishna's words in the Bhagavad Gita- *ehaiva tairjitha sargo*.

While Sri Aurobindo's metaphysical influence has been strongly acknowledged and accepted across the world, his followers recognize him to be the harbinger of a supramental consciousness that shall bring about a universal radical transformation and summon the dawn of a supramental human race. However, I have observed that understanding Sri Aurobindo completely is a conundrum for not just the ordinary folks like myself, but also for some of the extra-ordinary minds I have had the good fortune of meeting in life. I distinctly remember my interaction with one renowned scholar of great mental acumen who had devoted his life to researching Sanskrit scriptures. When I spoke about Sri Aurobindo's brilliant work on the symbolism of the Rig Veda, he gave a hearty laugh and said- "Reading Sri Aurobindo is not easy". Even among the devout admirers and followers of Sri Aurobindo, we find that something extra which is beyond intellectual ability is needed to understand the great master's works. In an interview on 27th May 1926, to Anilbaran Roy, Sri Aurobindo had replied when the former expressed that he had not the slightest clue of what the supermind was:

"What is required is faith. Man has body, life and mind but that is not all that constitutes man. He has risen to the mind as a result of evolution. Now a higher consciousness will be evolved – this I call Supermind. It is the instrument of the Divine Consciousness, the Truth-Consciousness."

- Sri Aurobindo

And that is why, as we undertake an attempt to delve into the newest Upanishad that the world received- Sri Aurobindopanishad, I ask you to take a leap of faith while entering into Sri Aurobindo's resplendent world of golden light. By taking a leap of faith in approaching his works you are by no means, being asked to enter into a covenant with Sri Aurobindo that will prevent you from questioning anything. You are merely being asked to put aside albeit temporarily, the effervescent contradictions that are likely to arise at the outset from the level of mental logic. It is like when the physicists enter into the quantum world, they are left with no option but to embrace the quantum concepts and put aside completely their rigid attachment to Newtonian laws.

Every question has its place, but logical questions cannot be used to gain supra-logical answers. And this is also the mind-set that is a perquisite when reading any Upanishad, for that matter, as all of them use the mind as mere spring board to jump into the planes beyond the mind and gain an entry into the kingdom of *Brahma* vidya. The mind is vestigial entity while dealing with the *Brahman* and this truth needs to be acknowledged and understood.

What you will find most intriguing about Sri Aurobindopanishad, the newest Upanishad that the world received is that Sri Aurobindo takes us into the kingdom of Bramhavidya in a such a smooth manner that we hardly realize when he shifts the gears from the physical to the metaphysical. Sri Aurobindo was known to meticulously answer the questions of the *sadhaks*, even while in the midst of his supramental sadhana, at times even spending 6-8 hours every day to correspond with and clear the doubts the various sadhaks would express when they wrote to him. This trait of Sri Aurobindo will be explicitly visible as we move through his Upanishad where he uses mental logic to gently nudge us into the experience of true bliss, *Sat Chit Ananda*, that comes when we become dwellers in the kingdom of *Brahma* vidya.

Before I present to you my poetic rendition of Sri Aurobindopanishad, which I believe may provide a little assistance to the reader in understanding Sri Aurobindo and his Vedanta, I am sharing the master's poem titled invitation,

"With wind and the weather beating round me
Up to the hill and the moorland I go.
Who will come with me? Who will climb with me?
Wade through the brook and tramp through the snow?

Not in the petty circle of cities
Cramped by your doors and your walls I dwell;
Over me God is blue in the welkin
Against me the wind and the storm rebel.

I sport with solitude here in my regions,
Of misadventure have me a friend.
Who would live largely? Who would live freely?
Here to the wind-swept uplands ascend.

I am the lord of tempest and mountain,
I am the Spirit of freedom and pride.
Stark must he be and a kinsman to danger
Who shares my kingdom and walks at my side"
- Sri Aurobindo

The First Movement: *The Principle of Brahmic consciousness*

The opening of any Upanishad is of great significance as it casts light upon the direction of the Upanishad. This is precisely why the *Isha Upanishad* or *Ishavasyopanishad* is itself named after the opening words – *Ishavasyam idam sarvam*. Sri Aurobindo's Upanishad can be categorized into four parts, based on four significant movements that take place in it.

This first movement clearly establishes the *Principle of the Brahmic consciousness*.

ॐ। एकमेवाद्वितीयं ब्रह्म सदसद्रूपं सदसदतीतं नान्यत्किञ्चिदस्ति त्रिकालधृतं त्रिकालातीतं वा सर्वन्तु खलु ब्रह्मैकं यत्किञ्च जगत्यामणु वा महद्वोदारं वानुदारं वा ब्रह्मैव तद् ब्रह्मैव जगदपि ब्रह्म सत्यं न मिथ्या।

स एव परात्परः पुरुषस्त्रिकालातीतः सकलभुवनातीतः सकलभुवनप्रविष्टः सदतीतोऽसदतीतः सन्मयश्चिन्मय आनन्दमयोऽनाद्यन्तः सनातनो भगवान्।

स निर्गुणो गुणान्धत्ते सगुणोऽनन्तगुणो निर्गुणत्वं भुङ्क्ते स्वयञ्चातिवर्तते निर्गुणत्वञ्च सगुणत्वञ्च न निर्गुणो न गुणी केवल एव यः।

स भुवनातीतो भुवनानि धारयति भुवनभूतो भुवनानि प्रविशति कालातीतः कालो भवत्यनन्तः सान्तः प्रकाशत एको बहवोऽरूपो रूपी विद्याविद्यामय्या चिच्छक्त्या।

स्वयन्तु न धर्ता न धार्यो नानन्तः न सान्तो नैको न बहुर्नारूपो न रूपी केवल एव यः।

सर्वाणि त्वेतानि नामानि यदेकत्वञ्च बहुत्वञ्चानन्तञ्च सान्तञ्च प्रकाशन्त एव चिदात्मनि चिन्मये जगति।

ॐ

Om, He is the Brahman,
The singular non-dual One-
In all the forms that persist,
And also in those that do not exist.
He is beyond the existent,
Transcending even the nescient! 6

Nothing else ever existed or can without Him be-
In the Past, Present or Future in the worlds three.
Every creation- whether high or low in stature,
Wide or narrow, micro or macroscopic in nature.
All is He and He is One
The singular Brahman! 12

He is the truth- the highest that can be attained,
In his creation too- the same truth is contained.
This is the Brahman's truth supreme
Which is not false even in the mortal realm!
Beyond all three times, eternal and transcendent,
He is the Divine-omniscient and omnipresent! 18

He is the embodiment of truth consciousness,
Spread across the universe's vastness.
A bliss of pure ecstasy without end or beginning,
He is the ancient Divine- all pervading.
To Him – no qualities can be attributed,
And yet within Him all qualities are constituted 24

Despite holding qualities immeasurable and countless
He enjoys the experience of being quality-less!
It is Himself that He transcends,
And beyond the limits of qualities, He extends.
Neither devoid nor possessing any qualities in particular-
This is His nature Divine and singular. 30

The universe with all the worlds is His manifestation,
And He forays into His own worldly creation.
Though He is time's constant component,
Transgressing time, He is also its proponent!
His opulence radiates from the infinite-

And projects into the material finite.36

The formless one who to varied forms conforms,
Ignorance and Knowledge are but his two forms.
He is neither the bearer nor is the borne,
Neither a infinite nor finite, He is the unknown.
The formed One who holds forms none
Not Singular, not plural, and yet "The One" 42

The Finite, the Infinite, the One and the Diversiform
Are all but the multifarious names of His universal form.
Of consciousness and spirit that illuminates-
The entire world with the consciousness it generates
For such is its conscious luminance
That in its created world too reflects its brilliance 48

The opening lines of Sri Aurobindopanishad invite us to first deliberate upon the physical form of the Brahman who is described as the One who is not two but is many. While this may seem puzzling to the logical mind that cannot digest the topic of changing forms, one can very well tame it by bringing to mind the biology of a known and very much existing form changing prokaryotic entity- *chaos diffluens* or *amoeba proteus*. While the Brahman need not conform to our understanding of a typical primitive unicellular or advanced multicellular organism, our common knowledge prevents us from altogether rejecting the very concept of a form changing existence.

The next attribute is the omnipresence of the Brahman. The Brahman is present in all the creatures, irrespective of whether they are macroscopic or microscopic in nature and no existence can be deemed to be of a higher or lower stature when we recognize that the same Brahman is in all. In fact, the very existence of life is not a factor that the Brahman is dependent upon as the Brahman's presence is in non-living entities too. This all-pervading Brahman cannot be pinpointed to any particular location on the face of the earth and this attempt at tracking the position of the Brahman logically warps the limits of the three dimensions of space. Inextricably linked to these three spatial dimensions is a fourth dimension of time or '*kaala*' in what is recognized as the space-time continuum. This leads us to the possibility of the Brahman's ability of not only warping the boundaries of form and space but also being capable of transgressing time. While the concept of an entity capable of making holes or tearing the space-time fabric seems impractical, the possibility of such an existence cannot be altogether denied if the conditions of omnipresence are met. This gives us a third attribute to the definition of the Brahman. The form changing Brahman who is omnipresent is also a master of *kaala* or as Sri Aurobindo uses the word '*trikaalatit*' meaning beyond the three times of past, present and future.

As all these dimensions of space and time belong to the world, we can very well see that the Brahmic existence belongs to the world when when the Brahman portends within the limits of time and space and is otherworldly when the Brahman extends beyond time and space. And this is further clarified by the verse "*Jagadapi Brahma, Satyam na Mithya*" which mean that the Brahman is in the creation too, and this is true and not false.

We have come across the principle of energy which can neither be created nor destroyed and which is always in motion undergoing transformation. Energy is identified in Sanskrit as Shakti and the Brahman is considered as the creator of this energy or *Chit shakti* or consciousness energy. This gives us the fourth and final attribute of the Brahman being pure consciousness energy.

Thus we have, from the first movement of the Upanishad, pieced together the Sri Aurobindonian principle of *Brahmic* consciousness

The Brahman is the omnipresent existence, formed and formless, both at the same time, dwelling in and transcending the dimensions of time and space, permeating the entire cosmos and found in all the entities, living or non-living whatsoever, whose worldly presence for matters of human perception can be termed as –Chit - or pure consciousness.

At this conjecture, let us with a broad mind, accept for purpose of proceeding ahead into this Upanishad, this principle which will serves as a stairway to move into the next movement of the Upanishad

The Second Movement: *The Sun of Truth*

Now that we have accepted the principle of the *Brahmic* consciousness, we have earned ourselves a pass into the resplendent and golden kingdom of Brahma *vidya*. But just as an adventurer foraying into a new country needs inputs from a local guide to become accustomed to the niceties of the alien land, we too will need a hand to initially wade around in the kingdom of Brahma vidya. Since ancient times, if at all there is a manual that can serve as guide to understanding the Upanishads, it is the Bhagavad Gita. It is so time tested and accurate that the Gita is also termed as an Upanishad in itself, often revered as Gitopanishad.

Krishna in the XVII Adhyay, which is the penultimate chapter of the Gita, uses this very formula as a key to unlocking the Vedic wisdom, and passes it on to Arjuna in the middle of the battle field, while empowering him to not forsake the world or his duties towards it. The sincere hearted Arjuna, had entered into an utterly depressive mode after realizing that his enemies were the ones he had wanted to save. With love and a patience, that is truly divine, Sri Krishna brought back Arjuna into the world after displaying to him the light that powers the sun and all the greatest lights in the world, *jyotisham api tad jyotih* and a confident Arjuna finally uttered to Krishna that he had chosen his way of life in the world.

This contextual significance of the Gita is very much necessary not just because this movement opened with the triple mantra but also because in this movement we see Sri Aurobindo very succinctly teaching us the two concepts of Maya and Leela that are otherwise very difficult to grapple with.

ॐ तत्सत् यच्च सच्चिदेव तच्चिन्मयं जगद् भासते चिदात्मनि सत्यप्रकाशः सत्यस्य भगवतः।

यथा सूर्यस्य प्रतिबिम्ब एकः शान्ते जले बहवश्चले सत्यः सूर्यः सत्यः प्रतिबिम्बः सत्यप्रकाशः सतः सूर्यस्य न स स्वप्नः सतः प्रकाशस्तु सः। यथा वा सूर्यस्य ज्योतिः सौरं जगत्स्वशक्त्या धावदिव पूरयत्प्रकाशते सत्यं ज्योतिः सत्यप्रकाशः सतः सूर्यस्य न सोऽलीका भातिः सतः सत्यप्रकाशस्तु सः। यथा वा सूर्यस्य ज्वालामयं बिम्बं न स्वयं सूर्यः सूर्यस्य तु सूर्यत्वं प्रकाशयत्येतदन्नमयं रूपमन्नाश्रिते ज्ञाने तद्रूपातीतस्तु सूर्यः सत्यः सूर्यः सत्यं रूपं बिम्बाकृति सत्यप्रकाशः सतः सूर्यस्य न स मायाचित्रं सतः सत्यप्रकाशस्तु सः।

तथेदं जगद्ब्रह्म सत्यप्रकाशो भगवतो न स्वप्नो न मायाचित्रं नालीका भातिः सतः सत्यप्रकाशस्तु तद् न स्वयं भगवान् तथापि स्वयमेव सः। एषा परा मायैषा योगमाहात्म्यं रहस्यमयस्य योगेश्वरस्य कृष्णस्यैषा चिच्छक्त्या आनन्दमयी लीला परस्यातर्क्या गतिः।

सर्वमिदमर्थतः सत्यं परार्थतः असत्यमिति मनस्तुष्ट्यर्थं विज्ञानार्थमुच्यतां न हि किञ्चिदप्यसत्यं सत्ये ब्रह्मणि।

एवं यत्प्रकाशते जगदानन्द एव तत्।

Om tat sat- That truth is for sure!
Whatever that truth is, that alone is consciousness pure.
The world of consciousness in the spirit's consciousness persists-
Which is the divine truth- the real light that exists.
Like the image of the sun in silent waters singly reflects
And in turbulent waters, multiple reflections it projects; 54

The sun, the image and the light are all physically real
They are true, not a part of a dream- virtual and surreal
Just as the sun, though running, by its own light is powered
And by the same the solar system is illumined and empowered
The light is real and real is its luminance

Emerging from the real sun, which isn't pseudo-radiance.

The brilliance that is real emanates
From a sun that is real- it originates.
The blazing structure of the sun is but a perception,
Not the sun itself, but that which is understood by the human cognition
Its but a physical form which by the senses is perceived
Of the sun whose light, from a yonder sun is received.

The sun that is the blazing ball of fire too is the true one
And its light is the true light of the real sun
This isn't an illusion but is the truth authentic and reliable.
As the sun is real and this truth is undeniable
Likewise is the Brahman, the light of truth and divinity
Not an illusion (Maya) or a creation of mental activity

Not a false luminance, a mirage or a trick of light
But is the experience of the real truth's insight
Thus the sun is not the Divine One
But the divine Himself is the sun
This world is the illusive web supreme
Spun by the divine Himself in the mortal realm

The divine karma of Sri Krishna- the mystic Lord of Yoga
All is His song of blissful consciousness- His Leela.
All of this is true in the understanding
But actually is not in the working
For the reasoning mind's satisfaction, it is true
And to it, other than this- All is untrue.

But to the illumined mind, the integral truth is understood
That the Brahman is real and in Him there is no falsehood
And all that exists in this worldly creation
Is but Leela- His worldly blissful manifestation.
The light and Bliss in existence -
Is naught but the experience of His presence!

We see, in this second movement, Sri Aurobindo aiding us to delve further into the Upanishadic truth of the Brahman using some of the concepts of the Gita. It opens up with the triple formula of the Gita- Om tat sat

Many aeons ago, this triple formula was conceived-
By the same sacrifice, the Vedic knowledge was received-
The mantra "Om tat sat" with-Om the primordial syllable
Tat the eternal Brahman, Sat is the highest truth cognizable.|17.23|
- Sushrut Badhe, Bhagavad Gita: Rhythm of Krishna,
Canto XVII, P 23.

Continuing on this ground, we see Sri Aurobindo invoking the triple formula of 'Om tat sat' and declaring that this consciousness which is identified as the Brahman is a fundamental truth in existence and the entire world thrives in this consciousness.

To simplify the phenomenon of the Brahman, Sri Aurobindo brings to us the imagery of the physical sun and its reflection in the water. When you stand by a river front in the early hours of the dawn, what do you see?

The beautiful sun and its image is reflected in the waters. When there are no ripples on the surface, we see a singular reflection. When the water is disturbed we see multiple reflections of the same sun in the water. What we see when we are awake is not an illusion or a dream but very much a real experience that is perceived through our senses by us. While our senses are definitely finite in their capacity of perception and what we perceive is but a distilled experience of reality, we cannot deny that we are experiencing a reality, even if it may be deemed to be only an infinitesimal portion of the ultimate reality. This is, I believe, the argument that is being proposed to us through Sri Aurobindo's imagery of the sun. The one sun that reflects singly in water becomes many when the water is disturbed. The sun is real and its reflection too is real and the light that is emanating from the sun, which is also visible in its reflections, too is real.

The physical sun rotates about its own axis and generates its own light which dispels the darkness and is the foundation of life in our solar system. The luminosity and radiance of the sun that is perceived in the physical world too is real. Now after establishing that the sun is real, Sri Aurobindo prods us to see beyond the physical sun to what lies yonder. This is where the transition into the kingdom of Bramha vidya begins. We are invited to look at the spiritual sun whose consciousness manifests as the physical sun. The symbolism of the sun has been extensively used by the ancient Indian rishis in the Rig Veda and also the Upanishads. In the 50 th sukta of the First Mandala of the Rig Veda, the spiritual sun of illumination is invoked and praised-

The peoples of the distant world perceive
Through the rays, the God they verily see
Blazing like the flames of the fire|1.50.3|

O Surya, your light, you cause all to acquire
You direct the world to become resplendent,
And the world too reflects your light refulgent|1.50.4|

- Sushrut Badhe, Rhythm of the Veda: Know your Devas, Soura Suktam, P 58.

The symbolic meaning of the sun representing consciousness can be clearly understood in the Isha Upanishadic verses 3, 9 & 12 where the sun is connected with light of knowledge and ignorance is identified with darkness or tamah. Where there is no light of knowledge, there is only the darkness of ignorance and such a realm was called sunless, 'asoorya'

asuryā nāma te lokā andhena tamasā vṛtāḥ |
tāṁs te pretyābhigacchanti ye ke cātmahano janāḥ ||3||

Post death, the doomed sunless realms they attain
Wherein only a blind darkness the beings can obtain
For this is the fate of those beings who kill
And pollute their souls by their own will.|3|

The Vedic seers recognized the physical sun to be a manifestation of a spiritual consciousness that was in the form of a sun but beyond the physical sun. They not only recognized the divinity of the sun but also arrived at several scientifically significant truths with a great deal of accuracy without sacrificing the spiritual significance of the Sun. Most scientists are still finding it mind boggling to learn how the Vedic Indians arrived at accurate astronomical figures about planets and their movements aeons before the first telescope was invented. Science was never a casualty in the pursuit of the spirit and the Rishis clearly recognized the inseparable oneness that fused matter and spirit in the universe.

"The Solar energy is the physical form of Surya, Lord of Light and Truth, it is through the Truth that we arrive at Immortality, final aim of the Vedic discipline. It therefore under the images of the Sun and its rays, of Dawn and day and night and the life of man between the two poles of light and darkness that the Aryan seers represent the progressive illumination of the human soul"

– Sri Aurobindo, Vol15,CWSA P289

The blazing ball of fire that we understand to be the physical sun is real indeed and this truth is undeniable. All life on earth is powered by the sun's rays and all life flourishes and progresses sunwards and this is the truth of this creation. This is not some play of lights or an illusion but is a very fundamental truth of existence in this world. Sri Aurobindo calls this fundamental truth the *Brahman* and the truth of the Brahman is not an illusion or *Maya*. It is but an intelligent design of a supreme consciousness and Sri Aurobindo calls it a *Leela*- a dvine song of the Sri Krishna, who is the Yogeshwara- the lord of the union. This is a beautiful allegory to the golden words uttered by Sri Krishna -Himself, in the song of God, Bhgavad Gita, where Sri Krishna describes to Arjuna that his Divine consciousness is at work behind the scenes in the word and this is the divine working of the universe. This is crystal clear when we see the verses,

janma karma cha me deviyam

He who understands My birth-Divine
And knows the way of My Divine works
After death his consciousness merges into Mine
And he relapses not into the cycle of endless births.|4.9|

Krishna in the Gita in this verse reveals to Arjuna that whoever understands the divine's existence in the world and the functioning of the divine behind the veil of things attains to the highest consciousness that is free of death, which is the immortal consciousness of the Brahman.

This is *Maya*- the illusion Divine-
That engulfs every creation of Mine.
Crossing over beyond the veil can very hard be
But only by surpassing it can one approach Me!|7.14|

While this liberation is humanly possible, there is a veil of illusion that prevents man from realizing this act of God, the divya karma that is in progress in our everyday life. This is Maya, the game of illusion that has been put in place by the Divine and Krishna says in the Gita that we have to pierce through this veil to realize the Brahman supreme. He even explicitly mentions that this realization can be got here itself, *ihaiva tairjitah sargoh.*

It is clear as daylight, that the Brahman who has conceived the creation has also embellished the creation with His presence. If we still have some remnants of our logical mind that still attempt at mocking or pricking us with logical questions such as how can we believe that a God of union is wanting to unite us after separating us from Him, let us look at this from our lens of science, tinted with the finite limitations of our mental logic, one last time before we remove it permanently to get a pristine and unhindered view of our world.

This world's origin, as science currently believes and understands as a reliable cosmological theory, began with an explosion or a big bang. According to it, a huge and bright star exploded, scattering pieces of itself across the galaxy and formed a sun. The particles of that star which separated began cooling and formed planets that began revolving around the the broken star that continued to emit light. This became the sun and all the planets that consequently began to receive the light became a part of the solar system. The various elements combined and fused under various conditions of temperature and pressure and ultimately life was born on our planet earth. Materially we too were one with that supreme star before the big explosion. We were once upon a time emitters of light and now we are receivers of the same and we grow because sun light powers our every physiological functions.

The Vedic rishis were no different in their cosmological understanding as well. The universe originated with an explosion, a great Brahmic sound, the nada Brahman which they called 'Om'. And after this was a differentiation of a one consciousness which began spreading and separating from its origin, as the Upanishadic *mahavakya- ekoham bahusyami*. They called this separation- *viyogah* and recognized that this too was a game, a leela of the Divine to bring about a union- *Yoga*. When we look at this logically too, we find ourselves marvelling at the surreality of this undeniable truth of existence.

And as we reconcile with this truth, the divine game that is at play in the world becomes visible to us and when we truly realize our part in this game, we rise in consciousness. Away from the, illusion or maya that is foisted upon us, which prevents us perceiving the grand game of forces that is at play in the universe. It is only when we understand this, we can become conscious participants of the game that has already been set into play by the divine- the leela.

We don't remain entrapped in a lower nature that continually binds us into sense bound alternating experiences of happiness and sorrow and we consciously tend to move beyond these fluctuations of emotions into a more stable experience of a bliss that is unperturbed by the outer occurrences. This is what the Vedic Rishi's called '*Ananda*' and this is also where Sri Aurobindopanishad takes a decisive turn. We move into the next moment where Sri Aurobindo elucidates the game of light and shadow, *Ananda* and *Niranda*.

The Third Movement: *Ananda & Nirananda, A Game of Light & Shadow*

As we move into the third movement of this Upanishad, we grow closer into understanding 'Ananda' – the undiluted and unadulterated bliss that is the culmination and final check point of the divine game that is at play in the universe. This bliss was the immortal nectar that the Rishis of the ancient times sought fervently and to reach it, the individual had to break free from the clutches of nature. While '*Prakriti*' was always recognized as the nature component of the Purusha's (suprmere Brahman) divine consciousness and revered as an executive power of the divine, the Rishis were very clear in their perception that Prakriti was not altogether perfectly manifested in the world. They understood that Nature was manifest with the divinity and also the aberrations, *vikaaras*- as Krishna speaks in the Gita, which acted as the pitfalls in the divine game of Ananda. In the Gita, Sri Krishna describes these aberrations to be ensnaring in nature. When one gets attached to them, he gets entrapped in Maya's web of darkness or tamas. In the 15 th Adhyaya, he describes this design to be akin to an eternal and ethereal tree of life

From its roots above, seeded in eternity
And branching below, is the ethereal *Ashwattha* tree
The many hymns of the Vedas are but its leaves
He who knows this, the essence of Vedas he perceives.|15.1|

Above and below the cosmic tree's branches extend,
In the material and supra-physical planes they portend,
Raised by nature's qualities and their derivative senses
Roots of bonded actions into the mortal world it dispenses|15.2|

This inverted *Ashwattha's* form on earth is inconceivable
Neither beginning nor end nor foundation is perceivable
With the sharpest sabre of detachment alone can one sever
And escape from its roots that entangle the being forever.|15.3|

With detachment alone, could one could become free from darkness and only those who had mastered the game of darkness and light where able to progress into the supreme state that was only pure Ananda, an ecstatic delight. Beyond the dualities, the Suprme One, *ekameva advitiyam* as Sri Aurobindo aptly puts in the opening words of this Upanishad, the light that lights the sun becomes visible to the mortal who has transcended into the state of pure bliss.

For there, the timeless resplendent One comes to sight
Whose radiance is beyond the fire, the moon or the sun's light
They return not after having journeyed the distance
For they reach the zenith of the status of My existence. |15.6|

With these opening remarks, let us move into the third movement of this Upanishad, which again begins with the triple formula of the Gita, Om tat sat:-

ॐ तत्सत् यच्च सच्चिदेव तद्यच्च चित्स आनन्दः। यत्तु निरानन्दमिति भासते दुःखमिति दुर्बलमित्यज्ञानमिति तदानन्दस्य विकार आनन्दस्य क्रीडा।

यो हि जीवः स आनन्दमयः प्रच्छन्नो भगवान् स्वप्रकाशमयं जगद्ब्रह्म भोक्तुमवतीर्णः। य एष दुःखभोगः स भोग एवानन्दमयस्तस्यानन्दमेवानन्द-मयो भुङ्क्ते।

को हि निरानन्दं भोक्तुमुत्सहेत यः सर्वानन्दमयः स एवोत्सहेत निरानन्दमयस्तु निरानन्दं भुञ्जानो न भुञ्जीतानन्दं विना प्रणश्येत्। को दुर्बलो भवितुं शक्नुयाद्यः सर्वशक्तिमान्स एव शक्नुयाद् दुर्बलो ह्याक्रान्तो दुर्बलत्वेन न तिष्ठेच्छक्तिं विना प्रणश्येत्। कोऽज्ञानं प्रवेष्टुं समर्थो यः सर्वज्ञानमयः स एव समर्थोऽज्ञस्तु तस्मिंस्तिमिरे न ध्रियेतासत्त्वसदेव भवेद् ज्ञानं विना प्रणश्येत्। ज्ञानस्य क्रीडाज्ञानं स्वस्मिन्नात्मगोपनं शक्तेः क्रीडा दौर्बल्यं निरानन्दमानन्दस्य क्रीडात्मगोपनं स्वात्मनि।

सानन्दं हसति जीवः सानन्दं क्रन्दत्यश्रूणि मुञ्चति तमोमय आनन्दे भासमान इव यातनाभिश्चेष्टमानः सानन्दं स्फुरति सानन्दं स्फुरति चेष्टमानः प्रचण्डाभी रतिभिः। पूर्णभोगार्थं तस्यानन्दस्य तामसस्यांशस्य तामसो भूत्वा-नन्दं गोपयति।

Om tat sat. (Om This Truth)
Whatever is truth, that is consciousness
And this consciousness is the zenith of blissfulness (Ananda)
What is termed suffering, misery and weakness
Is but ignorance, a vacuum devoid of true happiness
All that is sorrowful is naught but true bliss's deviation
And in the play of divine bliss, an aberration. 96

When the Brahman into His illumined world extended
His life form of bliss- Jiva into the creation descended
In every soul to participate in the joy and sorrow that persists
Yet experiencing and enjoying all as bliss- He exists.
Who is He? O So eager to experience suffering?
Only He who possesses the bliss of everything. 102

To him without bliss, the experience of sorrow can't hold attraction
For devoid of happiness, such a being only attains destruction.
Who is it who can dare choose to become weak?
Such a desire only the all-powerful can afford to seek.
For if the weak, into further weakness diminish 108

Devoid of strength, such beings will only perish
Who can boldly foray into a state of ignorance?
Only He who exists in the state of omniscience
Ignorance is only ignorance and cannot blight darkness further
Without knowledge it is destroyed altogether
Ignorance is but the light of knowledge's play
And knowledge conceals itself in ignorance this way114

Weakness is when strength is concealed in a similar ploy
Likewise sorrow manifests when bliss veils itself in its own joy
The Jiva laughs and experiences its joys of birth,
Shedding tears, it cries and suffers too in mirth
A dark shadow of bliss, it blares and palpitates
And in different tortures and torments, it blissfully participates120

It is only to revel in Ananda's dark shade

Into oblivion the Jiva does verily wade. 122

'Om tat sat', the triple Vedic formula used by the Rishis to meditate upon the highest truth is invoked by Sri Aurobindo to help us connect with the supreme consciousness. He states that the highest truth was naught but pure consciousness which is the greatest experience of a natural and the highest ecstatic delight that a human can perceive. But he points out to us that the human experience is wrought with misery, weakness, suffering. Sri Aurobindo clearly states that Ignorance or '*tamas*' is the reason for all the unfavorable human experiences. '*Tamas*' can be looked at from two point of views; the individual and the cosmic level.

On the individual level, ignorance is the sole reason why we have these painful experiences. While this does seem diametrically opposite to the commonly uttered phrase "Ignorance is bliss" that is so often repeated to gloss over one's mistakes, it is in fact the main reason why we experience suffering. When we look at it on a deeper level, we can see that ignorance is actually a pseudo-bliss and this pseudo-bliss too is temporary. Ignorance can give a temporary happiness which lasts only until karma catches up and gives us a taste of the consequences of our own acts of ignorance.

On the cosmological level though, *tamas* has different significance even though it is an aberration which is born out of a distortion in the grand design that was set into play right at the inception of the universe. Sri Aurobindo explains that when the Brahman illumined the world with his consciousness and light, a portion of his consciousness too entered the universe to become life – *Jiva* in its myriad forms. And during this entry, a distortion took place and created ripples in the creation. This can be better understood if we look at the phenomenon of the dispersion of white light into the various spectral colours when passing through the medium of a prism or a diffraction grating.

Sri Aurobindo states that this movement of the Brahman was a conscious one where the all-powerful Brahman consciously chose to descend into His own creation. Since the *Brahman* is already in a state of Ananda, the ripples in his creation do not disturb his state of bliss. Only the all blissful can consciously choose to experience a state of non-bliss or *Nirananda.* If we look at this, on the individual level too, we see a similar logic. Only one who is truly and completely happy, can consciously choose to experience and understand what sorrow is. But the individual who is already sorrowful cannot choose sorrow as he is already in that state and if he were to choose to descend into further sorrow, that would end up lowering his consciousness further and further until it ultimately destroys the individual.

In a very similar manner, only the individual who is all powerful and strong can choose to become weak. The weak cannot make this choice and if the weak consciously becomes weaker, the individual would only perish. In the similar manner, only the omniscient One can dare to venture into a state of ignorance by hiding his own omniscient light from the world by a hood of darkness. The one who is already in pitch darkness cannot become more dark, the only possible movement from the nadir of darkness is an upward movement towards light.

This is the modus operandi of the *Brahman*, who conceals His own strength by a garb of weakness, his own light of knowledge with a veil of darkness. So Sri Aurobindo asks us to look beyond this veil and tells us that weakness is but a ploy where strength is concealed by itself. Sorrow is but happiness hiding its own self with a mask of sadness. Darkness too is naught but light hiding itself in its own shadow. The *Jiva-* life form that is present inside each individual is in a constant state of bliss, even though the outer individual goes through the experiences of sorrow, pain and suffering due to the various outer torments and tortures it has to experience in the game of the *Prakriti.*

This is very much in consonance with the teachings of the Gita as well! Sri Krishna in the XIII Adhyaya on the 'The Knower, The Field and its divisions' describes *Prakriti*, the Divine nature as the counterpart of the Divine in the game of the *ParaBramhan Purusha:-*

The domino of cause and effect is Her procreation
The experiences of individual consciousness, Her creation.
And the one supreme being- The Purusha does but enjoy
Experiencing both pleasure and pain with joy.|13.20|

Immersed in Her qualities, He presides
Experiencing Her nature, He resides

His attachment to Prakriti is the sole cause
Of all births in mortal wombs of sin and good that He draws|13.21|

Situated within this physical envelope mortal
Is the one supreme indwelling Lord immortal
He is the witness, observer and giver of consents
Nature's modes He enjoys, upholds and augments.|13.22|

He who knows and realizes the duality-
Of the supreme Purusha and Prakriti's every quality
His way of living or actions notwithstanding-
That being certainly finds release from rebirth's bonding.|13.23|

The Gita too talks about this cosmic game at play in the universe, with the two main players being the Purusha and His divine counterpart in Prakriti-Prakriti. Sri Aurobindo very succinctly teaches us this Vedantic principle, calling upon us to look beyond the shadows into light, beyond the pain and identify the hidden bliss and find the strength which is concealed in the garb of weakness. This movement teaches us to recognize the game of Ananda and Nirananda, that of shadow and light which is constantly at play in the universe. With this understanding, we are ready to move into the final movement of Sri Aurobindopanishad.

The Fourth Movement: *The Celestial Adesh: Collective Moksha*

This moment contains the Adesh – Divine instruction of Sri Aurobindo. However, before we look into it, it is essential to understand why Sri Aurobindo's words can be considered to be an authority when it comes to the domain of Vedanta.

Just like how in today's times, before a research article is accepted for its research value, editors first vet its literature survey to see if the author of the article has used reliable sources or evidences which are accepted universally, while formulating the hypothesis; the ancient Rishis too had evolved various systems of authentication & evaluation of the various hypotheses on the *Brahman.* The first of them was the system of *mimamsa* which encouraged critical investigation and exploration of the deep concepts of the Vedas. The evidences that were considered acceptable were called *Pramana* and these were accepted as reliable means of knowledge for framing a hypothesis on the Brahman. Prominently, the *pratyaksha* –direct experience of wisdom through spiritual experience, *anumana-* the deeper inferences that one draws from studying it, *arthapatti–* what one can derive from its circumstantial evidence, *anupalabdhi–* elimination of that which is unconceivable and the *Shabda-* the source that is indisputably considered to be authentic and reliable

If one were to study Sri Aurobindo's life from the point of his sudden withdrawal from active politics in pursuit of an arduous *sadhana* or spiritual practice for several decades in quest of the supramental manifestation, one cannot ignore reading the *pratyaksha pramana* available in the form of the various spiritual realizations he penned.
If we are unable to accept the direct experience of wisdom of his experiences, skimming through the several volumes of critical literature that he wrote on the Vedanata will give us the necessary base to accept his authority in the field of *Brahmavidya.* Personally, I find Sri Aurobindo's writings to be a *shabda pramana* as I feel his words echo and re-inforce the teachings of the Bhgavad Gita, which has over

the several thousand years since it came into being, attained a status of the *Pramana Shastra.*

Those who cannot bring themselves to accept Sri Aurobindo's spiritual realizations, any which way, face the uphill and impossible task of dealing with and trying to negate or disprove his written words. It is much easier to find a needle in a haystack than to find faults or negate the truth in the words found in his books as every statement of his is backed by a profound and enlightened understanding and wisdom. In fact, the task is so cumbersome that a renowned spiritual cult leader resorted to hurling insults and advised his followers to not read Sri Aurobindo, giving irrational arguments that Sri Aurobindo's logic was too convincing or that his biggest fault is that he never contradicted himself! Such an argument is neither mystic or scientific and it doesn't hold ground and the legacy of Sri Aurobindo has only spread over the years and it is no wonder that all of India is celebrating the 150th year of Sri Aurobindo's birth this year.

The readers may be very interested to note that Sri Aurobindo had his life transformational Krishna experience of '*Vasudevam sarvam iti'* in the jail. Quoting it in his own words,

"I looked at the bars of my cell, the very grating that did duty for a door and again I saw Vasudeva. It was Narayana who was guarding and standing sentry over me. Or I lay on the coarse blankets that were given me for a couch and felt the arms of Sri Krishna around me, the arms of my Friend and Lover. This was the first use of the deeper vision He gave me. I looked at the prisoners in the jail, the thieves, the murderers, the swindlers, and as I looked at them I saw Vasudeva, it was Narayana whom I found in these darkened souls and misused bodies....
.....I looked and it was not the Magistrate whom I saw, it was Vasudeva, it was Narayana who was sitting there on the bench. I looked at the Prosecuting Counsel and it was not the Counsel for the prosecution I saw; it was Sri Krishna who sat there, it was my Lover and Friend who sat there and smiled."

-Sri Aurobindo

Now let us turn tow what Krishna says in the Gita, verse 7.19

बहूनां जन्मनामन्ते ज्ञानवान्मां प्रपद्यते |
वासुदेव: सर्वमिति स महात्मा सुदुर्लभ: ||7.19||

After many successive births can this fortune arise
When the divine is percieved through mortal eyes
Very rare and blessed indeed is that seeking soul
That experiences the Divine omniscience as a whole. 7.19

Here, Krishna describes the experience of the divine in all objects, animate and inanimate, as a very rare spiritual experience of a pure and realized soul and called it to be a mark of a *Mahatma.*

Now, doesn't the experience of Sri Aurobindo in prison, sound mightily similar to what is indicated in the Gita. This only re-imposes our faith in the sanctity of Sri Aurobindo and his spiritual quest.

For the benefit of the readers, I have rendered a poem, in first person, of the experience of Sri Aurobindo in jail:-

Dearest, a prisoner I was in a lone cell
Alone, my pain I couldn't share or tell
With a deathly noose hanging atop
My life's aspiration, fate tried to stop
Hunger and thirst began blaring signs of defeat
I lay confined in a cage- six by nine feet

A year passed, I wondered is this the end?-
Of the leader, the symbol, the legend?
A barrage of thoughts left me mad-
"Why God?" was the burning question sad.
But all the inner turmoil and noise
Faded as I summoned an inner poise

And dearest, you taught me lessons three
That ultimately only set me free!
The first at the borders of insanity
I found the vista of the inner clarity
Next, beyond the limits of the mind
A higher tranquillity I could find

And finally how personal effort was a blunder

Without a complete and Divine surrender
Now, Suddenly in the dingy cage all was fine
I began to experience a Life divine
For everywhere, i only saw your face's reflection
How your majesty's beauty was beyond human comprehension 24

As a child in the universal mother's bosom
A new spiritual realization began to blossom
The walls now began to crumble and fall
I could now clearly see the One veiled in all
Dearest "Krishna, Vasudeva, Narayana"- how should I call?
Visible you became even in the Bars and the wall 30

Dearest I found you, as you simply surrounded me
And saw how no cage could now bind me
Walking under the branches I came to know
How you were cocooning me in your shadow
The rods and grating of the prison cell
Were also you i could smile and tell 36

I saw how you were standing sentry
Guarding dutifully the cage's entry
The course blankets too as your arms became
For in them i could feel the beloved's touch and name
In the other inmates, swindlers and murderers too
In all the misused bodies too I only saw you 42

As I used the vision that you gave me
Why I was imprisoned I could clearly see
Celebrating your gift of the divine sight
I tasted your ambrosia of ecstatic delight
The realms beyond the mind were now clear
New horizons have now begun to appear 48

"It was the hour before the gods awake"
Dearest, my supramental plunge I shall now make 50

This Sri Krishna experience was a transformational one as it changed the entire course of Sri Aurobindo's journey. From being in the heart of Politics, in the freedom movement of India, he withdrew as per the *Adesha*-celestial command that he received from the Divine. Quoting his own words from the famous *Uttarpara* speech on the 30th of May, 1909 at Bengal,

Then in the seclusion of the jail, of the solitary cell I asked for it again. I said, "Give me Thy adesh. I do not know what work to do or how to do it. Give me a message." In the communion of Yoga two messages came. The first message said, "I have given you a work and it is to help to uplift this nation. Before long the time will come when you will have to go out of jail; for it is not my will that this time either you should be convicted or that you should pass the time as others have to do, in suffering for their country. I have called you to work, and that is the adesh for which you have asked. I give you the adesh to go forth and do my work."

- CWSA Vol. 08Karmayogin

And it was this *Adesha* that Sri Aurobindo undertook. We see Sri Aurobindo in this Upanishad, written years after the *Adesha* he received in the prison, being true to the advice and celestial command that he received and we see him using this text as a means to relay onto the readers the sacred instruction that he received directly from the Divine in the final and concluding part of this Upanishad text.

अज्ञानं मूलमेतस्य भावस्य सान्त एवाहमहमशक्तो दुर्बलो दुःखी मया कर्तव्यं ज्ञातव्यं लब्धव्यं प्रयासेन तपःक्षयेण मृत्युना स त्वमेषोऽहं यत्त्वं न तदहं यत्तव शुभं तन्ममाशुभं येन तव लाभस्तेन मम हानिः त्वामेव हन्यां सुखी भविष्यामि नैव सात्त्विकोऽहं त्वामेव सुखिनं करोमि स्वदुःखेन स्वहान्या स्वमृत्युनेत्याद्यज्ञानस्य स्वरूपं मनसि।

अहङ्कार एव बीजमहङ्कारमोक्षादज्ञानमोक्षः अज्ञानमोक्षाद् दुःखान्मुच्यत आनन्दमयोऽहं सोऽहमेकोऽहमनन्तोऽहं सर्वोऽहमिति विज्ञायानन्दमयो भव-त्यानन्दो भवति।

एष एव मोक्षः। स मुक्तः सर्वेषां भोगान्भुङ्क्ते सर्वानानन्दाननन्तं भुञ्जानो न सान्तैर्वियुज्यते सान्तानि भुञ्जानो नानन्तेन हीयते स एको भवति बहुर्भवति स ह्यजो जायत इव जायमानोऽपि न जायते न बध्यते न जन्म तस्य विद्यते आत्मन्यात्मात्मना प्रकाशयाम्यात्मानमिति ज्ञानाद् विमुक्तः क्रीडते।

लीलार्थं हि जगदानन्दार्थं लीलामय इति लीलां कुरुतानन्दस्य पुत्राः मुक्ताः क्रीडतानन्दं भुङ्क्तैकं भोग्यं भगवन्तं प्राप्य भुङ्क्त सर्ववस्तुषु।

आनन्दं हि प्रवक्ष्यामि भगवतादिष्टः। तामसमपावृत्यानन्दः प्रकाशतां तस्य पुत्राः।

"I am depressed, weak and with much limitation"-
Ignorance is the root cause of this misconception.
"Through actions I have to toil, exert and perform,
As only to a perishable mortal nature do I conform.
He and I – we aren't one. I am not He!
This is my nature. He and I can never same be! 128

Whatever is good for Him, is to me bad
He has only rejoiced and gained in every failure that I had
In His destruction alone is my joy and emancipation
In my death and my sorrow is his celebration"
And other similar pejorative thoughts you will find
When ignorance takes control over the mind. 134

Ego is the root cause and also the seed

Which causes ignorance to surface and lead
When from ego the being finds release
Ignorance too in all forms begins to cease
And when the being is rid of ignorance
From all sorrows, one gains deliverance.140

"I am the embodiment of the bliss divine
I am that, The One and Infinite in all that is fine"
When by the 'Jiva' – this knowledge is attained.
A life of unending bliss is forever gained
This is moksha – the final liberation
Thus liberated the being enjoys the state of salvation146

In all experiences he realizes a bliss infinite
Relishing the finite in the infinite and the infinite in the finite
Despite being one, many forms he assumes and takes
Though Himself birthless, in innumerable births he partakes
Becoming all, the fulfilment of countless births he attains
And yet his birthless original nature still remains 152

He is the unborn and he cannot be bound
His 'Self' illumines Himself, spreading the light around
In this illumined consciousness, He forever stays
With this detached knowledge, he freely participates and plays
This world is naught but His play divine
His Lela, created to enjoy all that is fine 158

O Children divine, in this joyous play partake
The bliss of creation; enjoy, experience and take
Unite with Him, seeing Him in all become one
Celebrate this bliss highest, that is comparable to none.
Under the command celestial, I verily pronounce
The way to the blissful consciousness, I thus announce164

"O Children of bliss, harbingers of His celestial light
Removing darkness, With His bliss divine,
Set the world alight!"166

ॐ

In the beginning of the third movement, Sri Aurobindo clearly stated that our individual experiences of suffering, misery and weakness are only out of ignorance. In this final movement, Sri Aurobindo describes how ignorance takes control of the individual's thought process

First the individual begins to feel like an abject failure when the individual's ego is unsatisfied. He begins to feel like he is weak and limited and depressing thoughts take control of the individual. The divinity within and outside of the individual begins to feel like plain falsehood. This is followed by paranoia where the individual begins to feel disgust and resentment towards the divine and all things divine and the individual comes to believe that the divine takes sadistic pleasure in the destruction and loss of the individual. Sri Aurobindo identifies the root cause for individuals having a state of mind where one cannot recognize divinity quite bluntly. He says that it is ego which is the seed and the root for such type of thoughts.

But when one sheds this ego, the cloak of ignorance just disappears and one is free from the suffering and the realization of one's own innate divinity comes to the individual. This *sakshatkarah* – which is the Sanskrit word for a complete realization of one's own true self is the aim of the spiritual practice and the destination that all spiritual seekers have been seeking since Vedic times and when this comes to the individual, man becomes divine. This phenomenon of becoming conscious of one's own divinity is the liberation from the cage of suffering, the moksha, the salvation that is possible in this birth itself.

Lokmanya Balgangadhar Tilak planted the hero's fire into the hearts of people of all ages, in India's freedom revolution, with his slogan – *"Swaraj is my birth right and I shall have it"* and this became an anthem for the quest of the independence of India from several years of slavery. In Sri Aurobindo's own words, Lokmanya Tilak was- '*one who built much rapidly out of little beginnings, a creator of great things out of an unworked material. The creations he left behind him were a new and strong and self-reliant national spirit, the reawakened political mind and life of a people, a will to freedom and action, a great national purpose.'*

Sri Aurobindo too after recognizing the need for a future revolution, withdrew from active politics only to light the beacon for the next movement that was to take its grip in India. In the 75th year of India's independence, in the 150th year of Sri Aurobindo's birth, the time is now ripe for a 'consciousness revolution'. Borrowing the quote of Tilak Maharaj, in Sri Aurobindo's light, may we live this slogan from within and without - *"Sakshaatkarah is my birth right and I shall have it".*

It is only when we become conscious of truth, the falsehood of ignorance will truly leave us in our life. And in this state of consciousness, the transformation from an ordinary life to a 'Life Divine" will take place. While the very concept of an individual human being attaining the highest realization, *moksha*, in his own lifetime without having to leave the world does sound quite radical, it is not very different from what Krishna tells us in the Gita:-

Unhappiness in all its forms ends
And all sorrows, away this blessing sends.
Filling the seeker's mind with ethereal joys
He attains the perfect wisdom's poise |2.65|

Bereft of pride and delusion, with a desire-less detachment
Embedded in the Self, by conquering the fault of attachment
Having surpassed the dualities of joy and sorrow for good
The enlightened ones progress towards the status of Godhood.|15.5|

He who is able to bear and sustain,
The rush of anger and the gush of desire
In this very birth itself he shall obtain-
The highest realization of bliss that man can acquire.|5.23|

The sages of the awakened Self are liberated and free-
For in their minds, no desire or wrath can unconquered be
For within themselves the Nirvana of Brahma they withhold
And around them-this realization in all directions they unfold. |5.26|

Where the mind is tamed by a disciplined will
By the awakened knowledge it is purified and still
And the one perceives the Self by the Self's gnosis
Thus dwelling in the state of the supreme Bliss |6.20|

Sri Aurobindo tells us that this realization of the divine is the Vedantic moksha and what makes his yoga, unique is that it casts light onto the possibility of moksha without rejecting the material world, a perfect reconciliation of man and divinity, matter and spirit which is the direction in which humanity is evolving. In the final and concluding part of this text, we see Sri Aurobindo passing upon an instruction too all with a fatherly love. He invites his children to embrace the world, with all its deficiencies and flaws and receive the light. He repeatedly calls upon the spiritual seekers to not forsake the world but to enjoy and participate in the bliss of creation and experience the divine joy of existence that can come only by living in communion with the divine.

To rise in consciousness is his golden invitation and we are invited to raise our consciousness so each one of us can experience the light of divinity in our lives while being grounded firmly on earth. There is pain and suffering in our world due to the darkness of ignronace and we need to get freedom from ignorance in all walks of life to learn to love and to live in a truly divine way.

He raises a clarion call to all of humanity addressing us as "anandasya putrah" children of Ananda or bliss and challenges to face the darkness head on with the confidence of the light within us and gives us the parting Adesha to receive the light from the divine and spread it across so humanity can receive a rain of bliss and light.

This call needs to be heard, not by our ears but by our heart. Sri Aurobindo has spoken about the Call in Savitri

"Heaven's call is rare, rarer the heart that heeds."
– Sri Aurobindo

I conclude with a poet's prophecy: -
The Clarion Call pierced through the first dark cloud
And every mortal ear, heard the sound clear and loud.
Ecstatic skies thundered flaunting the silver lining
Ushering moist blind eyes- "The Heroes are coming!".

ORIGINS: **Midam**

On 24th November 1996, Sri Madhusudan Damle received the word Midam deep in his meditation. He has described this reception as a literal vision of a descent of three letters "मि द म्". He grabbed a white chit and immediately penned them down with a red marker that was near him, lest he forgets the letters and thus Midam was first materialized. He even made a toran of the words Midam on a paper on the auspicious '*Bhoomi Pujan day'* and put it on the fence.

In 1999, he built his building with the name Midam etched on it and he meditated upon it for hours. Not wanting to himself attribute any meaning to it, over the next couple of years, he approached multiple Sanskrit scholars asking them to share the meaning of this word. Many commented that on shruti, Midam appeared like a maha-mantra of "I am that" but were not able to perfectly state. Some more years passed and Damleji held this mantra close to his heart, keeping it a secret.

One fine day, during intense meditation, he spontaneously called upon the divine asking the divine only to clarify the meaning and immediately he heard the voice- "Don't you know? It is short for "Miraravindashranam mama".

A dashakashra mantra where the first, fifth and tenth letters were respectively "मि द म्". Damleji was satisfied but still kept this a secret from the rest of the world. In 2011, During an auspicious moment of inspiration, Damleji gave Midam a symbol and significance and under his direction, his NGO began the journey for engaging in loka sangraha which birthed several projects like Krishna's Butter Project, Vedic Chants Intervention, Rhythm of Krishna, Learning through nature etc. All these projects though were positively impacting tens of thousands of people across the world, only a handful of individuals had joined the mission and all activities were freely undertaken without even taking donations.

In September 2024, inspired by the work of some senior citizens connected to the Sri Aurobindo ashram who were cleaning up the trash and litter that was being indiscriminately dumped on the beach, Damleji himself engaged in the beach cleaning to join the movement and consciously supported it and on 18th October 2024, he re-organized his NGO founding "The Midam Foundation" to smoothen mass participation and also governmental collaboration for manifesting collective change so all members and volunteers can work "united yet freely" in the spirit of Damleji's modus operandi of free union.

When Damleji first came to Pondicherry in 1988, he heard from many directly or indirectly that this mission of his was just a dream. Not paying heed to detractors, he only smiled and said *"They call it only a dream. Let us all join hands to make it a living truth"*

This become his motto and the dream is being born. He is never in a hurry of things, but when it comes to manifesting a divine will, he works God speed.

ॐ मिदम् ॐ

****

MIDAM FOUNDATION – OBJECTS

1.Revival of Education systems with Gurukul projects & working with like-minded individuals, NGOs, governmental and private institutions.

2.Creating & aiding projects and conducting research and receiving support for revival of Indian knowledge systems (IKS) in India using latest technologies like Artificial intelligence (AI) and also entering into research collaborations with governmental and non-governmental organizations NGOs, national and international educational institutions and organizations.

3. Research & development of personality development education modules for children and adults.

4. Supporting and advancing projects for Women empowerment and promotion of good health in children by supporting projects for helping underprivileged women, widows and children.

5. Creating and developing a place that can give a serene atmosphere for the advancement of religion, spirituality or yoga.

6. Providing Relief for poor, education, yoga, medical relief and conduct of free medical camps and also donations to individuals and other charitable organizations.

7. Aiding and creating projects for the preservation of environment projects, cleaning drives in cities and rural areas individually or in collaboration with various governmental departments and purchasing of machineries for cleaning of public places and construction of toilets, installations of bins and the likes after obtaining requisite governmental regulatory approvals.

8.Preservation of monuments & articles, places of historical importance.

9.Public awareness projects for promotion of individual well-being in society thorough medical and spiritual camps, blood donation drives, suicide prevention programs etc.

10. Providing education and education material and support in the form of grants and/or donations of books to deserving individuals and people irrespective of caste, creed, or religion.

11. Advancements of projects of Public utility and conduct of awareness drives and de-addiction camps for public and working towards elimination of addiction to narcotics, addiction to alcoholic substances.

12. Furthering the projects that advance the research or treatment of animals, development of sustainable practices and innovative methods for promoting agriculture, promotion of ayurveda and ayurvedic therapies in collaboration with organizations, individuals and government departments such as the department of drugs control, AYUSH etc.

13. Supporting shelter homes for the destitute and elderly, supporting special schools, homes and individuals working for the betterment of life for children with special needs, conduct of awareness and sensitization camps for parents of children with special needs and also general public.

14. Rehabilitation support to individuals, families or organizations during natural calamities or man-made tragedies.

If any of these resonate with you, please consider this as an invitation to unite and work together freely.

****

The aim of Midam symbolized

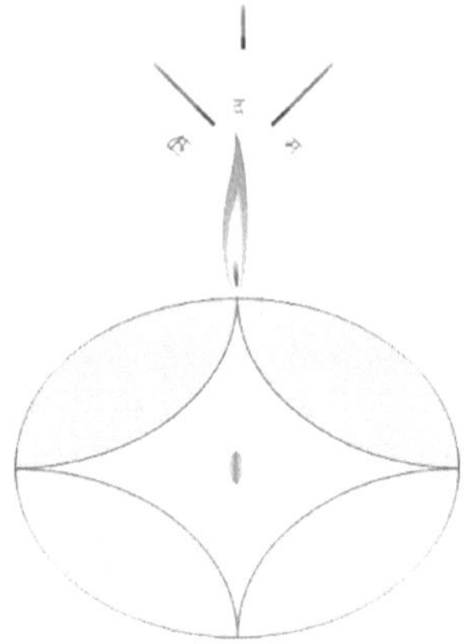

The sphere represents the earth that we live on.

The blue colour (upper hemisphere) depicts the skies and green (lower hemi-sphere) the flora and fauna.

The central yellow arched diamond represents man who is always in communion with the five elements.

Inside man is a tiny flame - the flame of aspiration which represents the *Chaitya Purusha* – "*the psychic being*".

Man's aspiration takes him higher and higher to meet the Supreme light represented by *Agni*- the flame.

This higher knowledge descends in man and he then embraces the earth having received this light- the knowledge, and he uses it for the betterment of all life on earth.

About the Author:

Sushrut Badhe (https://en.wikipedia.org/wiki/Sushrut_Badhe) is a mechanical engineer who primarily engages in the manufacturing of Ayurvedic products at his master's unit, KVM Research Labs (www.ayurvedaforyou.in). He engages in research related to Sanskrit scriptures and Indian Knowledge Systems (IKS) and has published papers in multiple reputed scientific journals like *International Journal of Religion and Health*, *Molecular Cytogenetics*, *Natural Language Processing journals*, *IEEE Access*, etc., and he has no idea why he does this.

He also has a good/bad habit of writing poetry in rhymes and likes using the name "Rhythm" in the titles of the books which he writes and releases for free. His books include *Rhythm of the Spirit*, *Rhythm of Krishna*, *Rhythm of Ananda: Sri Aurobindo's Vedanta*, and *Rhythm of Veda: Know your Devas*. Most of his books are available online at reasonable rates, but if you wish to procure a free PDF of any of his books, you can always send him a good old-fashioned email requesting a copy.

He believes his writing journey started ever since he got to meet his Guru, Sri Madhusudan Damle, during the ending months of 2010, and after he began residing with his Guru, the rhythm of poetry only grew. He also picks up trash (old alcohol bottles, wasted diapers, shoes, plastic spoons and more) as part of the "♥ Clean Earth, Together We Can!" group of conscious citizens who are taking the lead in cleaning up Pondicherry's rock beach.

Some words of request to the readers:

1. Please find your Guru in life (if you haven't found yours yet). This meeting can be a life-changing moment.
2. Please learn how to cook; it's very useful and necessary in life.
3. Have fun and enjoy with friends and family in the company of nature, if you wish, but please don't litter. I would love to have the superpower of picking up all of it with my own hands, but I am far too limited alone.

♥ Clean Earth, Together We Can.

The author may be contacted here

E-mail: sushrutayurveda@gmail.com

or

https://www.facebook.com/SushrutBadhe/